Andrew Brodie Basics
LET'S DO SPELLING

FOR AGES 8-9

with over **100** reward stickers

- Over 400 words to practise and learn
- Regular progress tests
- Extra tips and brain booster questions

Published 2014 by Bloomsbury Publishing Plc
50 Bedford Square, London, WC1B 3DP

www.bloomsbury.com

ISBN 978-1-4729-0861-2

Copyright © 2014 Bloomsbury Publishing
Text copyright © 2014 Andrew Brodie
Cover and inside illustrations of Comma the Cat and Andrew Brodie © 2014 Nikalas Catlow
Other inside illustrations © 2014 Steve Evans

A CIP catalogue for this book is available from the British Library.

10 9 8 7 6 5 4 3 2 1

Printed in China by Leo Paper Products

This book is produced using paper that is made from wood grown in managed, sustainable forests. It is natural, renewable and recyclable. The logging and manufacturing process conform to the environmental regulations of the country of origin.

To see our full range of titles visit **www.bloomsbury.com**

BLOOMSBURY

Notes for parents

What's in this book

This is the fourth book in an exciting new series of *Andrew Brodie Basics: Let's Do Spelling*. Each book contains more than four hundred words especially chosen to boost children's confidence in spelling and to reflect the demands of the new National Curriculum.

During the early stages of Key Stage 2, many children are confident in the skills of 'segmenting' (breaking words down to spell them) and 'blending' (combining sounds together to read whole words) and will apply these skills when learning the spellings in this book. Of course, some words don't follow regular phonic patterns so your child will need to learn these 'tricky words' by looking at individual letters and the general shape of the word.

How you can help

To get the most out of this book, take the time to discuss the activities with your child when there are no distractions around and they are in a responsive and enthusiastic mood. Talk through each of the practice words and what they mean by using them in spoken sentences, or by asking your child to make up sentences containing the words. Putting up posters of useful words around the house such as the days of the week and the months of the year, might also help with spelling generally.

To begin with, your child might find the spellings in this book quite tricky, but as they work their way through the activities and become familiar with the spelling patterns, their confidence should grow. The level of difficulty is increased gradually throughout the book but some spelling patterns are repeated to provide lots of opportunities for reinforcement and practice. Always be ready to provide plenty of encouragement and explain that they should learn from their mistakes rather than get disheartened.

Look out for...

Look, cover, write, check

Some pages feature 'Look, cover, write, check' exercises. Your child might have already come across this strategy in school. Ask your child to **look** carefully at each word, learning the shape of it and any letter patterns it contains. When they feel they know it, ask them to **cover** it with their hand or a piece of paper and to try writing it. They then look back at the original word and **write** it again to **check** that they really know it.

Comma the Cat

Look out for Comma the Cat who tells your child which words to focus on for the progress test at the end of each section. You could help your child to learn these words by posting them around the house on sticky notes or writing them on flashcards for quick memory games.

Brodie's Brain Boosters

Brodie's Brain Boosters feature quick extra activities designed to make your child think, using the skills and knowledge they already have. Some of these will ask your child to think of rhyming words. Don't worry if your child finds a rhyming word that doesn't match the spelling pattern of the given word. Use the opportunity to compare the spellings – looking carefully at words is, of course, the whole point of the activity!

The answer section

The answer section at the end of this book can also be a useful learning tool. Ask your child to compare their spellings with the correct spellings provided on the answer pages. If they have spelt the words correctly, congratulate them, but if they haven't, don't let them worry about it! Instead, encourage them to learn the correct versions. Give lots of praise for any success.

Singular and Plural

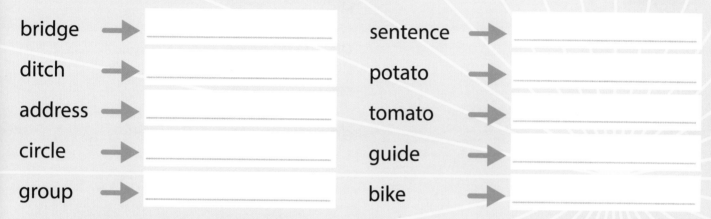

Remember singular is just **one thing** and plural is **more than one**.

To turn most words from singular into plural you just need to add an s, but for some words you need to add es.

Here's an example: the word cat is singular and the word cats is plural, but the plural of catch is catches.

Make these singular words into plurals.

bridge →

sentence →

ditch →

potato →

address →

tomato →

circle →

guide →

group →

bike →

Choose words from above to fit into the sentences below. Some of the words will be singular and some will be plural. Make sure you spell them correctly!

The helpful _____ showed us around the museum.

The _____ was cut up to make chips.

The Olympic champion rode her _____ really fast.

Gardeners like to grow juicy, red _____.

These _____ are not too difficult.

A _____ has no corners.

There are lots of _____ over the river.

Next to the road there was a deep _____.

Comma says…
Learn these words for your first progress test.

address   bridges

circle   ditch

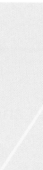

Words Ending in 'y'

For some words ending in y, you need to replace the y with i before adding es to make them plural.

Make these singular words into plurals.

baby ➡ _____

pony ➡ _____

ferry ➡ _____

hobby ➡ _____

daisy ➡ _____

century ➡ _____

To make these words plural you just need to add an s.

play ➡ _____

birthday ➡ _____

monkey ➡ _____

donkey ➡ _____

Comma says...

Learn these words for your first progress test.

babies   plays

hobby   monkeys

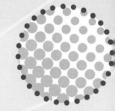

Choose words from above to complete the sentences below.

Five girls were riding _____ around the field.

In the last _____, people have travelled more and more.

Several _____ cross the Channel every day.

The noisy _____ was braying very loudly.

The children performed several _____ to the parents.

For some people, gardening is a _____; for other people it is just hard work!

My _____ is in January.

The _____ were jumping from one tree to another.

Sort the Words

Sort the words into singular or plural. Be careful: some of the words are spelt in exactly the same way, whether they are singular or plural.

mouse   house   strawberries   dishes   half   women

quarter   wolves   tooth   feet   sheep   catch   houses

mice   woman   deer   catches   strawberry   dish   foot

halves   quarters   wolf

Words that are spelt the same for singular and plural

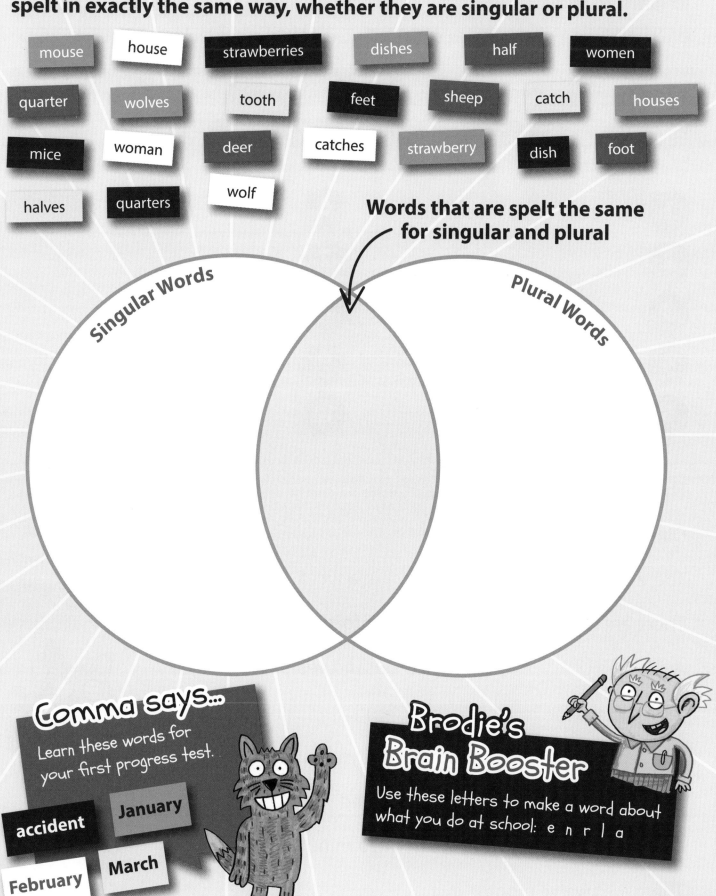

Singular Words

Plural Words

Comma says...

Learn these words for your first progress test.

accident   January   February   March

Brodie's Brain Booster

Use these letters to make a word about what you do at school: e n r l a

Time Words

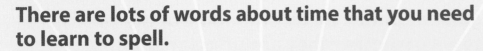

A second is a very short time.
A millenium is a very long time.

There are lots of words about time that you need to learn to spell.

Write these time words in order of size, starting with the shortest time.

century   month   second   year   week   day

minute   decade   hour   millenium

1 _____

2 _____

3 _____

4 _____

5 _____

6 _____

7 _____

8 _____

9 _____

10 _____

There are ten years in a _____.

Dinner will be ready in five _____.

There are seven _____ in a week.

There are two _____ in a fortnight.

A _____ lasts for a thousand years.

Each day is 24 _____ long.

The second _____ of the year is February.

A _____ lasts for a hundred years.

There are sixty _____ in a minute.

There are twelve months in a _____.

Comma says...

Learn these words for your first progress test.

seconds   months   century

Write the Words

Cover each word and see if you can write it without looking.
Then check and write it again.

LOOK (THEN COVER)	WRITE	CHECK
breath		
breathe		
appear		
disappear		
guard		
nature		
natural		
possible		
impossible		
thought		

Choose words from above to complete the sentences below.

We must take care of the _____ world.

We need to _____ all day and all night.

He _____ very hard about his work.

The _____ was looking after the jewels.

Freckles always _____
on my face in sunny weather.

Comma says...
Learn these words for your first progress test.

purpose medicine

difficult impossible

Use the words you have been practising to fill the gaps.

1. The doctor gave me some _____ for my cough.

2. There are four _____ across the river.

3. The bike ended up in a _____ at the side of the road.

4. Write the _____ on the front of the envelope.

5. A wheel has the shape of a _____.

6. The class performed three _____ in the hall.

7. I had an _____ and hurt my knee.

8. We go to school to _____.

9. The first month of the year is _____.

10. He didn't break the pencil on _____.

11. His _____ is to play football.

12. The _____ at the zoo were chasing each other in the tree-tops.

13. The shortest month of the year is _____.

14. _____ is the first month of spring.

15. Some maths is easy but some is very _____.

16. There are thirty _____ in half a minute.

17. There are twelve _____ in one year.

18. It's _____ to swim across the Atlantic.

19. There are one hundred years in a _____.

20. New _____ cry a lot at night.

Use the words you have practised.

Score _____ /20

8

Sort the Words

Some words are made from the same root word.

forgotten preferred gardener began youngest gardening

forgetting beginner ~~garden~~ forgot ~~prefer~~ ~~young~~

beginning ~~forget~~ ~~begin~~ younger

Sort the words into groups.

prefer

forget

garden

begin

Comma says...

Learn these words for your second progress test.

youngest forgotten gardener

beginning

young

Practise the Words

Cover each word and see if you can write it without looking.
Then check and write it again.

LOOK (THEN COVER)	WRITE	CHECK
gym		
gymnastics		
Egypt		
pyramid		
mystery		
young		
touch		
double		
trouble		
country		

Choose words from above to complete the sentences below.

My friend broke a glass and he was in a lot of _____ .

We went to Egypt to see a _____ .

I like watching _____ to see the gymnasts doing floor routines.

Some books are about a _____ .

Brodie's Brain Booster

Can you think of a word that rhymes with 'mystery', but which is spelt differently?

Comma says...

Learn these words for your second progress test.

gymnast

routine

shopkeeper

pyramid

Sort the Words

Read the words below.

expression   nation   possession   permission   admission   tension

expansion   mention   station   discussion   confession   question

extension   comprehension   position   emotion   intention   relation

prevention   punctuation

Copy the words on to the correct list.

WORDS ENDING WITH sion

_____

_____

_____

_____

_____

_____

_____

_____

_____

_____

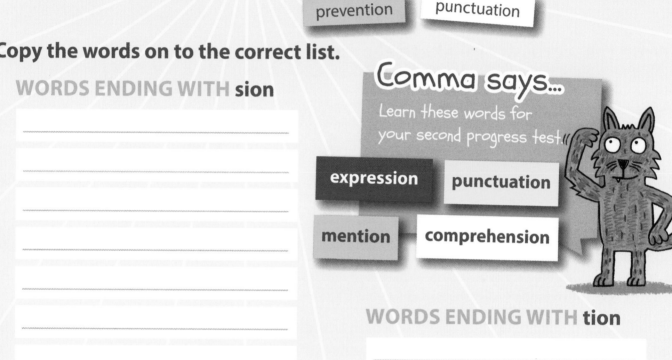

Comma says...

Learn these words for your second progress test.

expression   punctuation

mention   comprehension

WORDS ENDING WITH tion

_____

_____

_____

_____

_____

_____

_____

_____

_____

_____

_____

Brodie's Brain Booster

Can you think of a word that is an extension of the word 'nation'?

Alphabetical Order

Read the words below. Sometimes you need to look at the second letter of a word to work out alphabetical order.

busy won't brother badly water who lorry

wedding again parents person puddle any nasty

many about mostly medal needle noisy rolling

lucky key kangaroo really laughing

Write the words in alphabetical order.

_____ _____ _____

_____ _____ _____

_____ _____ _____

_____ _____ _____

_____ _____ _____

_____ _____ _____

_____ _____ _____

               _____

               _____

               _____

Comma says...

Learn these words for your second progress test.

parents laughing really mostly

Write the Words

Cover each word and see if you can write it without looking. Then check and write it again.

LOOK (THEN COVER)	WRITE	CHECK
accidental		
answer		
arrive		
believe		
bicycle		
build		
business		
calendar		
caught		
centre		

Choose words from above to complete the sentences below.

'I don't _____ a word you're saying,' said the policeman to the thief.

We have already bought our _____ for next year.

'Please _____ the question,' said the teacher.

'That's none of your _____!' said the girl crossly.

The train is due to _____ at eleven o'clock.

Comma says...

Learn these words for your second progress test.

bicycle   caught

centre   answer

Brodie's Brain Booster

Can you think of a word that rhymes with 'caught'?

13

Use the words you have been practising to fill the gaps.

Remember to check your spelling!

1 I am the _____ person in my family.

2 The town _____ is very busy.

3 My _____ are very kind to me.

4 The _____ sprang high into the air.

5 A _____ is a solid shape.

6 I forgot to _____ that I would be late.

7 She forgot to write any _____ in her sentence.

8 The man was _____ very loudly at the joke.

9 My _____ has two wheels.

10 I have _____ to feed the cat.

11 He had a very mean _____ on his face.

12 The _____ was cross when the customer knocked over a pile of cans.

13 Babies like a regular _____ every day .

14 The _____ was looking after his flowers.

15 I nearly _____ the ball but I dropped it.

16 The _____ of the story was very good but I didn't like the end.

17 I had to _____ twenty questions.

18 We had to read a short story then answer some _____ questions.

19 I like all types of sport but _____ I like football.

20 My teacher _____ likes me!

Score _____ /20

Sort the Words

Dogs and cats have four legs but we are NOT related!

Some words are related to each other because they have similar parts or similar meanings.

possible   disagree   beautiful   strength   strong   agreement

obey   beauty   obedient   possibly   disobey   honesty   disagree

honest   disobedient   strongly   agree   honestly   impossible   dishonest

Sort the words into groups.

beauty	obey

possible	
	honest

strong	
	agree

Comma says...
Learn these words for your third progress test.

strength   beautiful

honest   disagree

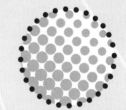

Write the Words

Cover each word and see if you can write it without looking.
Then check and write it again.

LOOK (THEN COVER)	WRITE	CHECK
marine		
submarine		
city		
intercity		
national		
international		
Superman		
superstar		
supermarket		
recycle		

Choose words from above to complete the sentences below.

We travelled on an _____ train.

I would like to travel underwater in a _____.

We sang the _____ anthem when the athlete won a gold medal.

I wish I could fly like _____.

Comma says...

Learn these words for your third progress test.

recycle   national

supermarke

submarine

Brodie's Brain Booster

Can you think of a word that rhymes with 'city' and is spelt in a similar way?

Pair the Words

Read the words on the list. Sort them into pairs where one word is the root word and the other word is an extended version of the root word. The first pair has been done for you.

~~serious~~ comical spontaneous curious complete hideous obvious

usual hideously finally ~~seriously~~ sad spontaneously

comically sadly obviously completely usually final curiously

---

serious
seriously

Comma says...
Learn these words for your third progress test.

obvious   comical

completely   finally

17

Alphabetical Order

Read the words on the list. Sometimes you need to look at the second letter of a word to work out alphabetical order.

section open under poison disaster behave
zinc enjoyment classic every zebra level
drawer laughter height interval stolen umbrella chase
impress grammar oven pattern bright guard history

Write the words in alphabetical order.

Comma says...

Learn these words for your third progress test.

grammar height section bright

Write the Words

Cover each word and see if you can write it without looking.
Then check and write it again.

LOOK (THEN COVER)	WRITE	CHECK
consider		
consideration		
continue		
continued		
continuing		
decide		
decided		
deciding		
difficult		
difficulty		
earth		
eight		
eighth		
experience		
experiment		
extreme		
famous		
favourite		
forward		
fruit		

Comma says...

Learn these words for your third progress test.

consideration   favourite

experiment   earth

Brodie's Brain Booster

Use these letters to make one word:
s i d l a n

Clue: Britain is one of these, because it has sea all round it.

19

Use the words you have been practising to fill the gaps.

Remember to check your spelling!

1 My _____ food is pasta.

2 The _____ went deep under the sea.

3 We sang the _____ anthem.

4 The squirrel looked very _____ when it was hanging upside down from the washing line.

5 The _____ is one of the sun's planets.

6 The sun is shining and it's a _____ day.

7 We have to learn about _____ in literacy.

8 My mum measures my _____ every month.

9 The moon is very _____ tonight.

10 Sometimes I _____ with my friend but we stay friends.

11 We did an interesting _____ in a science lesson.

12 "Show _____ towards other people," said the headteacher.

13 I was _____ exhausted after my race.

14 I thought the race was going on forever until _____ I saw the finish line.

15 The answer to the question was _____ to me.

16 We _____ all our plastic bottles.

17 Mum spent ages in the _____ .

18 "Everybody should be _____ with each other," said the headteacher.

19 I felt that I had lots of _____ to carry the bricks.

20 One _____ of the shop has clothes for sale.

Score ____ /20

Tricky Words

Dogs don't even know what suffixes and prefixes are!

Some words are made by adding suffixes or prefixes to a root word.

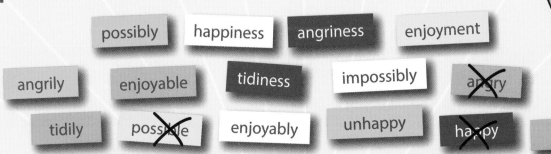

possibly   happiness   angriness   enjoyment

angrily   enjoyable   tidiness   impossibly   ~~angry~~

tidily   ~~possible~~   enjoyably   unhappy   ~~happy~~   ~~tidy~~

happily   unenjoyable   ~~enjoy~~   untidy   impossible

Sort the words into groups.

angry

enjoy

possible

happy

Comma says...

Learn these words for your fourth progress test.

enjoyable   tidiness

happiness   possibly

tidy

Practise the Words

Cover each word and see if you can write it without looking.
Then check and write it again.

LOOK (THEN COVER)	WRITE	CHECK
heard		
increase		
important		
knowledge		
naughty		
musician		
electrician		
magician		
politician		
mathematician		

Choose words from above to complete the sentences below.

Most children are good but they are _____ sometimes.

The _____ was talking on the television.

I asked for an _____ in my pocket money!

A _____ is very clever at maths.

We _____ a strange noise coming from the garden.

Comma says...

Learn these words for your fourth progress test.

naughty   important   musician   heard

Pair the Words

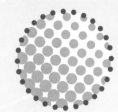

Read the words below. Sort them into pairs where one word is the root word and the other word is an extended version of the root word. The first pair has been done for you.

immature   relevant   impatient   inactive   ~~behave~~   incorrect

regular   correct   ~~misbehave~~   mature   legal   possible   irresponsible

illegal   irrelevant   impossible   responsible   patient   irregular   active

behave
misbehave

Comma says...

Learn these words for your fourth progress test.

regular   active

correct

patient

23

Alphabetical Order

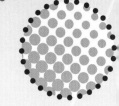

Read the words on the list. Sometimes you need to look at the second letter of a word to work out alphabetical order.

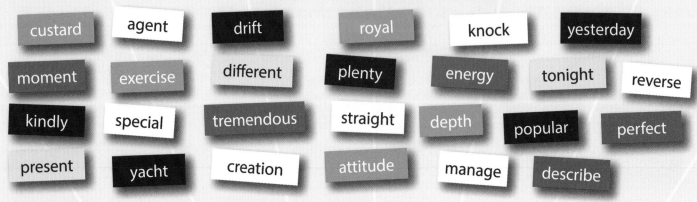

custard   agent   drift   royal   knock   yesterday

moment   exercise   different   plenty   energy   tonight   reverse

kindly   special   tremendous   straight   depth   popular   perfect

present   yacht   creation   attitude   manage   describe

Write the words in alphabetical order.

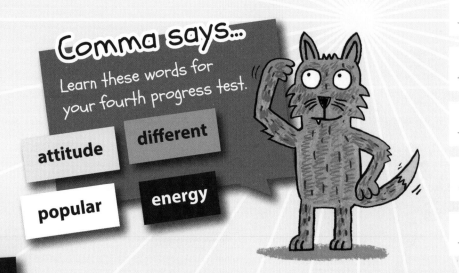

Comma says...

Learn these words for your fourth progress test.

attitude   different

popular   energy

24

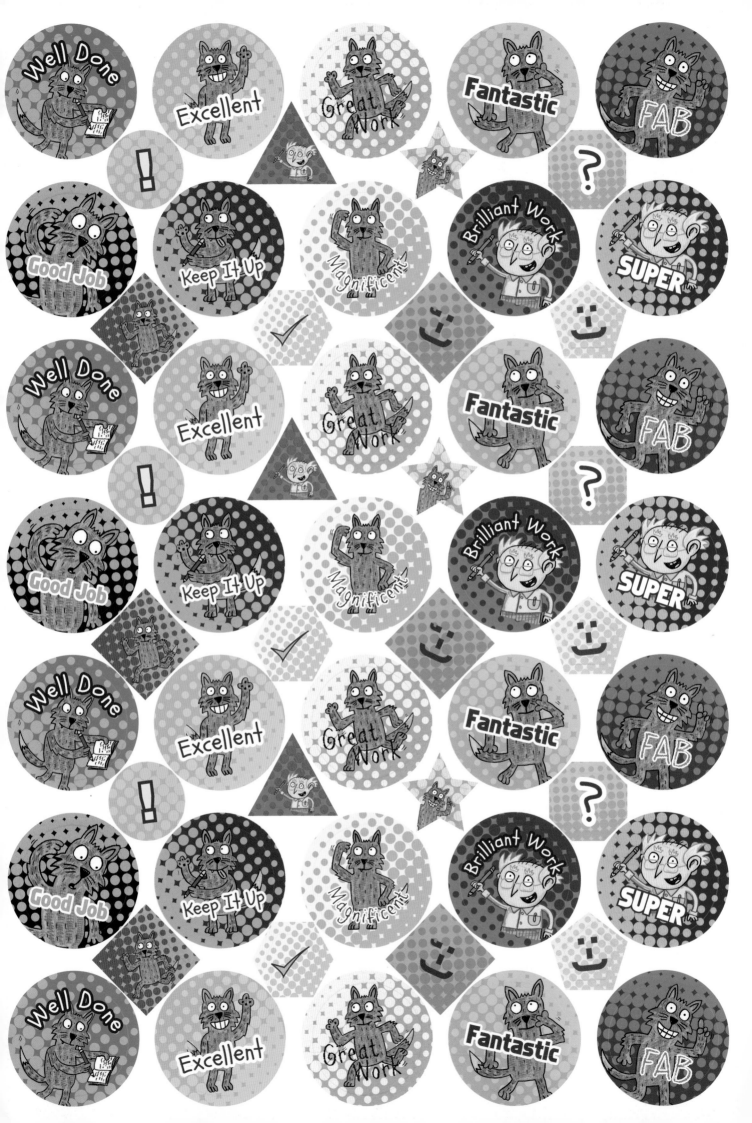

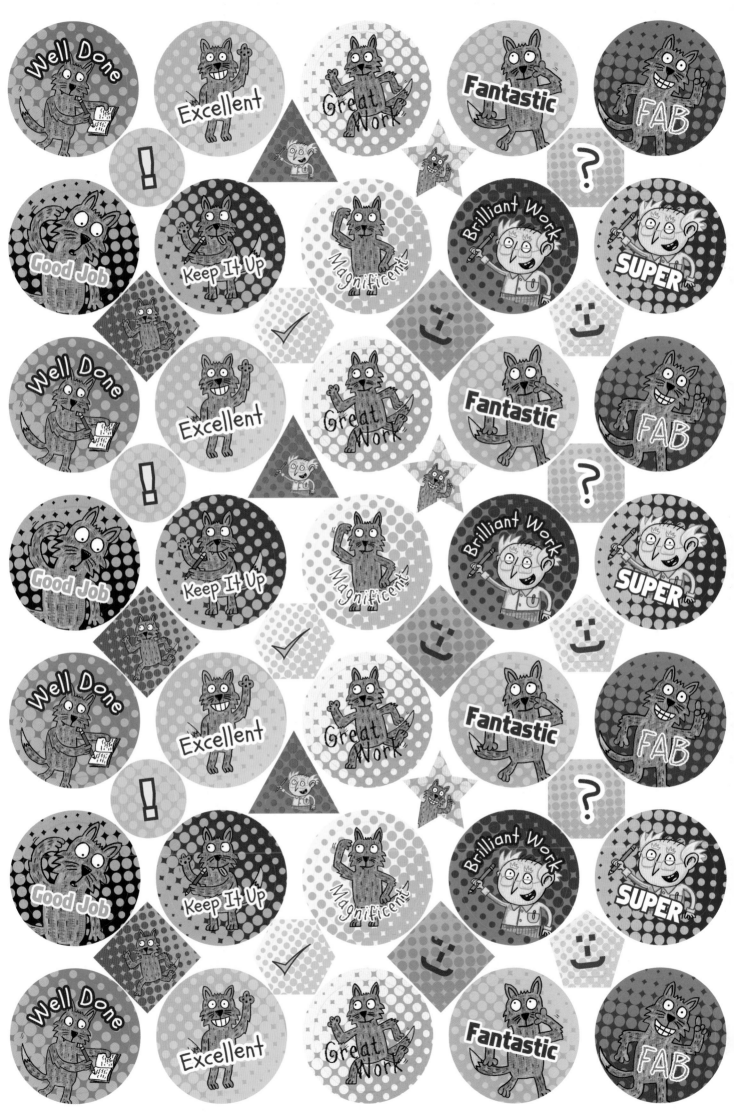

Write the Words

Always use your best handwriting!

Cover each word and see if you can write it without looking. Then check and write it again.

LOOK (THEN COVER)	WRITE	CHECK
particular		
particularly		
peculiar		
probably		
promise		
promised		
promising		
purpose		
purposely		
quarter		
recently		
regularly		
reign		
remember		
sentence		
separate		
strange		
strength		
suppose		
surprise		

Comma says...

Learn these words for your fourth progress test.

recently   **remember**

promise   **sentence**

Brodie's Brain Booster

Use these letters to make one word:
a c i t n o r f.
Clue: a quarter is one of these.

25

Use the words you have been practising to fill the gaps.

Remember to check your spelling!

1   My little sister is usually very good but sometimes she is _____.

2   A square is a _____ shape.

3   I couldn't _____ fly to the sun.

4   Some people don't care about the _____ of their rooms and some people do.

5   I made a _____ to telephone my friend.

6   It is _____ to spell correctly.

7   The _____ played the guitar brilliantly.

8   I would like to spread _____ to everybody.

9   I can't _____ how to spell every word.

10 "It's important to have a positive _____," said the headteacher.

11 Have you got enough _____ to climb this mountain?

12 I haven't been swimming _____.

13 "That's a very good roll," said the teacher. "Now can you show me a _____ one?"

14 I like to get all my spellings _____.

15 Some people are very _____ at school.

16 I had a really _____ day yesterday.

17 A _____ always starts with a capital letter.

18 Most teachers are very _____ with their pupils.

19 Some people like to keep very _____.

20 I _____ a cuckoo in the distance.

Score _____ / 20

26

Sort the Words

Dogs don't care whether they chase their tails in a clockwise or anticlockwise direction.

Remember that some words are made by adding suffixes or prefixes to a root word.

adoring shiny autograph ~~sense~~ clockwise ~~biography~~

sensing anticlockwise sensation informed adored autobiography inform

adoration informing sensed ~~shine~~ ~~adore~~ ~~clock~~ information

Can you sort the words into groups?

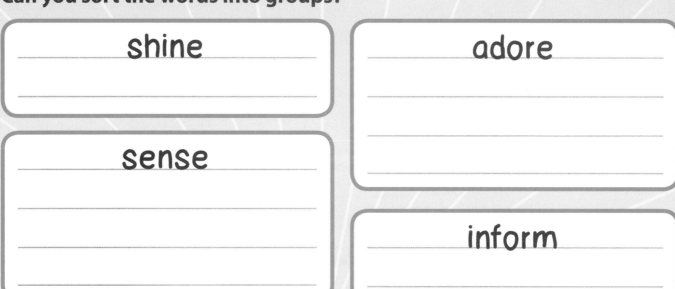

shine

adore

sense

inform

clock

biography

Comma says...

Learn these words for your fifth progress test.

clockwise adore

information shiny

27

Write the Words

Cover each word and see if you can write it without looking.
Then check and write it again.

LOOK (THEN COVER)	WRITE	CHECK
measure	_____	_____
measurement	_____	_____
treasure	_____	_____
pleasure	_____	_____
enclosure	_____	_____
creature	_____	_____
furniture	_____	_____
picture	_____	_____
nature	_____	_____
adventure	_____	_____

Choose words from above to complete the sentences below.

The pirate hid the _____ deep in a dark cave.

We had to move the _____ in the lounge to fit everyone in.

An ugly _____ came out of the swamp.

Our teacher asked us to _____ the length of the playground.

My favourite type of book has an _____ story.

Comma says...

Learn these words for your fifth progress test.

measure   **furniture**   **nature**   **pleasure**

Brodie's Brain Booster

Can you change the word 'nature' by adding a suffix to it?

28

Pair the Words

Read the words below. Sort them into pairs where one word is the root word and the other one is an extended version of the root word. The first pair has been done for you.

natural | humbly | frantically | ~~gentle~~ | basic | simply

septic | simple | dramatically | humble | noble | social | frantic

nobly | antiseptic | naturally | basically | dramatic | ~~gently~~ | antisocial

gentle gently	

Comma says...
Learn these words for your fifth progress test.

dramatically

simple

gentle

antisocial

Alphabetical Order

Read the words on the list. Sometimes you need to look at the second letter of a word to work out alphabetical order.

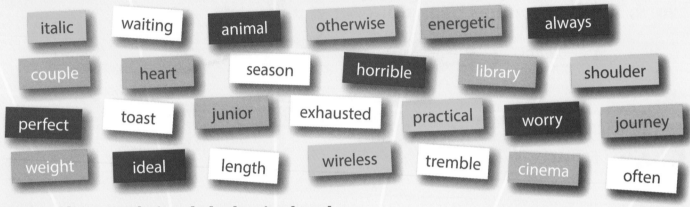

italic   waiting   animal   otherwise   energetic   always

couple   heart   season   horrible   library   shoulder

perfect   toast   junior   exhausted   practical   worry   journey

weight   ideal   length   wireless   tremble   cinema   often

Write the words in alphabetical order.

Comma says...

Learn these words for your fifth progress test.

library   junior

practical   cinema

Write the Words

Always use your best handwriting!

Cover each word and see if you can write it without looking. Then check and write it again.

LOOK (THEN COVER)	WRITE	CHECK
therefore		
though		
thought		
thoughtful		
thoughtfully		
through		
various		
variously		
weigh		
weight		
woman		
women		
occasion		
occasional		
occasionally		
weather		
whether		
rain		
rein		
reign		

Comma says...

Learn these words for your fifth progress test.

whether   **rein**

weather   **reign**

Brodie's Brain Booster

Can you think of a word that rhymes with 'thought'?

31

Use the words you have been practising to fill the gaps.

1   We need to look after every aspect of _____ .

2   The theatre school is split between senior and _____ students.

3   She was leading the horse by its _____ .

4   Queen Victoria had a very long _____ .

5   The _____ forecast said that it would be sunny later.

6   I don't care _____ it is sunny or not.

7   She spoke loudly and _____ .

8   The new car was very _____ .

9   Most mothers _____ their babies.

10   Mothers are very _____ when they pick their babies up.

11   I went to the _____ to choose a book to borrow.

12   We had to _____ the length of the field.

13   The water swirled in a _____ direction.

14   Some people are very friendly but some are quite _____ .

15   At first, the questions were _____ but the later ones were harder.

16   'I have great _____ in declaring the new school "open!"' said the Mayor.

17   We bought a table and some chairs and some other _____ .

18   I wonder what's on at the _____ .

19   I like writing, reading and maths but I also like _____ activities.

20   The children were looking for _____ for their history project.

Remember to check your spelling!

Score ____ / **20**

Sort the Words

Remember that some words are made by adding suffixes or prefixes to a root word.

~~complete~~   reaction   ~~invent~~   injection

inventor   ~~action~~   ~~inject~~   invented   ~~hesitate~~   inventive

hesitation   inventing   hesitated   completed   invention   injecting   hesitating

completion   inaction   injected   completely   completing

Can you sort the words into groups?

action

invent

complete

inject

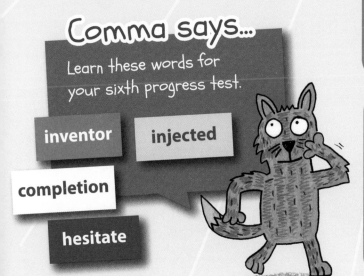

Comma says...

Learn these words for your sixth progress test.

inventor   injected

completion

hesitate

hesitate

Write the Words

Cover each word and see if you can write it without looking.
Then check and write it again.

LOOK (THEN COVER)	WRITE	CHECK
league		
tongue		
antique		
unique		
science		
scene		
discipline		
fascinated		
crescent		
neighbour		

Choose words from above to complete the sentences below.

My mum went into an _____ shop and bought an old chair.

Most of the teams in the _____ play their matches on Saturdays.

In our _____ lesson we had to check the temperature.

My next door _____ is very kind to me.

Comma says...

Learn these words for your sixth progress test.

tongue   antique

science   neighbour

Brodie's Brain Booster

Can you change the word 'unique' by adding a suffix to it?

34

Homophones

Words that sound the same but have a different meaning are called homophones.

Read the words on the list. Can you sort them into pairs of homophones? The first pair has been done for you.

~~berry~~   piece   meet   male   brake

plain   fair   mail   not   ~~bury~~   meat   break

main   meddle   plane   medal   mane

knot   peace   fare

---

berry
bury

Comma says...

Learn these words for your sixth progress test.

peace   piece

brake   meddle

Alphabetical Order

Read the words on the list. Sometimes you need to look at the second letter of a word to work out alphabetical order.

active whether sample cement notice diamond

scroll mistake lightning reduce pendant article

forehead natural conversation property youthful myself frighten

yearly launch timber weather during radio topical

Write the words in alphabetical order.

Comma says...

Learn these words for your sixth progress test.

notice

conversation

radio

lightning

36

Write the Words

Cover each word and see if you can write it without looking. Then check and write it again.

LOOK (THEN COVER)	WRITE	CHECK
scheme		
scheming		
chorus		
chorused		
choral		
chemist		
chemistry		
chemical		
echo		
character		
chef		
chalet		
machine		
machinery		
brochure		
decorate		
redecorate		
decoration		
decorating		
decorated		

Comma says...

Learn these words for your sixth progress test.

character   machine

chorus   decorate

Brodie's Brain Booster

Can you write the plural of 'chorus'?

Remember to check your spelling!

Use the words you have been practising to fill the gaps.

1 My next door _____ doesn't have any pets.

2 The doctor _____ the vaccine into my dad's arm.

3 The washing _____ made a very loud noise.

4 I didn't _____ that my mum had had her hair done!

5 The _____ was very proud of his invention.

6 It is not polite to interrupt a _____ .

7 'You can go out to break on the _____ of your work,' said the teacher.

8 The thunder clapped loudly, shortly after the flash of _____ .

9 The main _____ in my book is a girl of about ten years old.

10 I could taste the bitterness on my _____ .

11 'Don't _____ to call me if you need any help,' said the sales assistant.

12 I had a very large _____ of cake.

13 Most people want world _____ .

14 'Don't _____ with other people's affairs,' said the headteacher.

15 The car rolled down the hill because its _____ wasn't on properly.

16 Everyone joined in with the _____ of the song.

17 Mum bought an _____ vase.

18 I would like to _____ my bedroom.

19 People who are good at maths are usually good at _____ as well.

20 I heard my favourite song on the _____ .

Score /20

38

Sort the Words

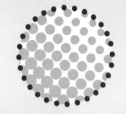

Suffixes are sometimes used to change the tense of words.

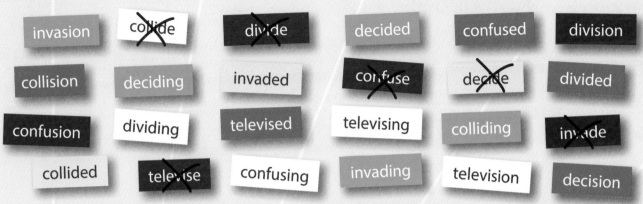

invasion · ~~collide~~ · ~~divide~~ · decided · confused · division
collision · deciding · invaded · ~~confuse~~ · ~~decide~~ · divided
confusion · dividing · televised · televising · colliding · ~~invade~~
collided · ~~televise~~ · confusing · invading · television · decision

Can you sort the words into groups? One set has been done for you.

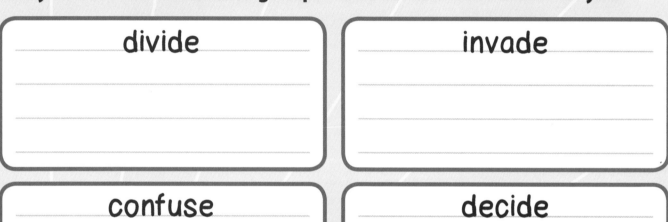

divide	invade

confuse	decide

Comma says...

Learn these words for your seventh progress test.

invasion · confusion · decision · televised

collide

televise

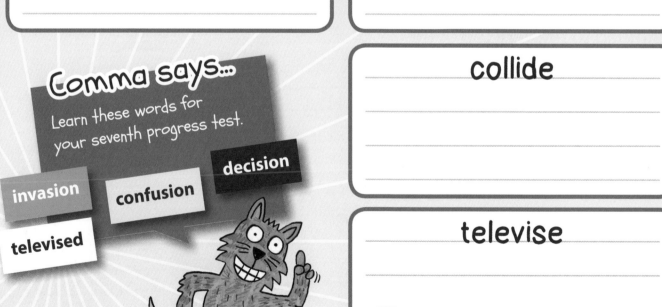

39

Practise the Words

Cover each word and see if you can write it without looking.
Then check and write it again.

LOOK (THEN COVER)	WRITE	CHECK
danger		
dangerous		
mountain		
mountainous		
fame		
famous		
various		
tremendous		
enormous		
jealous		

Choose words from above to complete the sentences below.

My sister was _____ when I had a new bike.

I climbed to the very top of the _____ .

The elephant was absolutely _____ .

I would like to be a _____
singer when I grow up.

Brodie's Brain Booster

Can you change the word 'dangerous' by adding a suffix to it?

Comma says...

Learn these words for your seventh progress test.

dangerous   jealous

mountains

enormous

40

Pair the Words

Read the words on the list. Sort them into pairs where one word is the root word and the other word is an extended version of the root word. The first pair has been done for you.

prepare · music · glamorous · courage · magic · admiration · vigour

usual · courageous · hum~~o~~rous · unusual · glamour · outrageous

vigorous · musical · magical · preparation · outrage · hum~~o~~ur · admire

> humour
> humorous

Comma says...
Learn these words for your seventh progress test.

prepare · unusual · humour · courage

Alphabetical Order

Brodie's Brain Booster

Can you add a suffix to the word 'discuss' to make another word?

Read the words below.

enough
artistic
yourself
ordinary
revise
middle

given
phoneme
runner
daughter
opposite
glasses

imagine
already
yawning
city
viaduct
pause
interesting

material
vocabulary
broken
complete
early
blackberry
discuss

Write the words in alphabetical order.

_____ _____ _____

_____ _____ _____

_____ _____ _____

_____ _____ _____

_____ _____ _____

_____ _____ _____

_____ _____ _____

_____

_____

_____

Comma says...

Learn these words for your seventh progress test.

yourself
material
artistic
interesting

Apostrophes

One dog's dinner is good for me to eat when he is not looking. Two dogs' dinners are even better.

Look carefully at these two sentences and notice how the apostrophe is used to show possession.

The sentences below include words with possessive apostrophes. Look carefully at how they are used. Write the words very carefully.

The man's car was rolling down the hill.

The men's cars were parked next to each other.

The woman's dog was barking very loudly.

The women's cats were purring quietly

The child's pushchair was bright red.

The children's pushchairs were all kept in the corner of the room.

The baby's teddy was well-loved.

The babies' teddies were all mixed up.

The girl's hair was tied in a ponytail.

The girls' changing rooms are upstairs.

The boy's bike was new.

The boys' bikes were piled in a heap.

Comma says...

Learn these words for your seventh progress test.

girl's   girls'

babies'   baby's

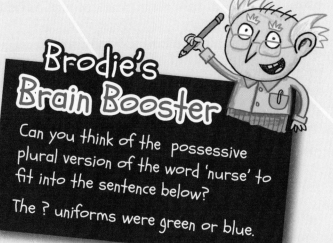

Brodie's Brain Booster

Can you think of the possessive plural version of the word 'nurse' to fit into the sentence below?

The ? uniforms were green or blue.

Use the words you have been practising to fill the gaps.

1 'Look after _____ !' said my grandmother.

2 The castle is _____ .

3 There was a bit of _____ to start with but now everything is clear to me.

4 I find wildlife really _____ .

5 The last _____ of Britain was in 1066.

6 Lots of sport is _____ so that people all over the world can watch it.

7 Mum used a scrap of _____ to mend my shirt.

8 The _____ hat has fallen off.

9 The _____ hats are over there.

10 My cousin is very _____ , so he spends all day painting pictures.

11 It is _____ to find oranges growing on trees in this country.

12 The _____ cot has lots of teddies in it.

13 The _____ mothers came to collect them from the nursery.

14 Everybody needs to have a good sense of _____ .

15 The long range of _____ in South America is called the Andes.

16 She showed great _____ when she rescued the man from the fire.

17 I was _____ when my brother got all the praise!

18 Rivers and canals can be very _____ .

19 I always _____ well for my spelling test.

20 I have made the _____ to practise even more spellings!

Score _____ / **20**

ANSWERS

Page 3 • Singular and Plural

bridges	sentences
ditches	potatoes
addresses	tomatoes
circles	guides
groups	bikes

guide
potato
bike
tomatoes
sentences
circle
bridges
ditch

Page 4 • Words Ending in 'y'

babies	plays
ponies	birthdays
ferries	monkeys
hobbies	donkeys
daisies	
centuries	

ponies
century
ferries
donkey
plays
hobby
birthday
monkeys

Page 5 • Sort the Words

Singular words:	Plural words:
mouse	strawberries
house	dishes
half	women
quarter	wolves
tooth	feet
catch	houses
woman	mice
strawberry	catches
dish	halves
foot	quarters
wolf	

Overlap contains:

sheep, deer

Brain Booster:

learn

Page 6 • Time Words

second	month
minute	year
hour	decade
day	century
week	millennium

decade
minutes
days
weeks
millennium
hours
month
century
seconds
year

Page 7 • Write the Words

words written as neatly as possible

natural, breathe, thought, guard, appear

Page 8 • Progress Test 1

1. medicine	11. hobby
2. bridges	12. monkeys
3. ditch	13. February
4. address	14. March
5. circle	15. difficult
6. plays	16. seconds
7. accident	17. months
8. learn	18. impossible
9. January	19. century
10. purpose	20. babies

Page 9 • Sort the Words

preferred	forgot
	forgetting
gardener	forgotten
gardening	
	began
	beginning
	beginner
	younger
	youngest

Page 10 • Practise the Words

words written as neatly as possible

trouble
pyramid
gymnastics
mystery

Brain Booster:

history or any other rhyming word

Page 11 • Sort the Words

Words ending with 'sion':	Words ending with 'tion':
expression	nation
possession	mention
permission	station
admission	question
tension	position
expansion	emotion
discussion	intention
confession	relation
extension	prevention
comprehension	punctuation

Brain Booster:

national, nationally, or any other appropriate word

Page 12 • Alphabetical Order

about	lorry	person
again	lucky	puddle
any	many	really
badly	medal	rolling
brother	mostly	water
busy	nasty	wedding
kangaroo	needle	who
key	noisy	won't
laughing	parents	

Page 13 • Write the Words

words written as neatly as possible

believe
calendar
answer
business
arrive

Brain Booster:

taught, bought, or any other rhyming word

Page 14 • Progress Test 2

1. youngest
2. centre
3. parents
4. gymnast
5. pyramid
6. mention
7. punctuation
8. laughing
9. bicycle
10. forgotten
11. expression
12. shopkeeper
13. routine
14. gardener
15. caught
16. beginning
17. answer
18. comprehension
19. mostly
20. really

Page 15 • Sort the Words

beautiful	obedient
	disobey
impossible	disobedient
possibly	
	honesty
strongly	honestly
strength	dishonest
	agreement
	disagree

Page 16 • Write the Words

words written as neatly as possible

intercity
submarine
national
Superman

Brain Booster:

pity, or any other rhyming word

Page 17 • Pair the Words

comical, comically
spontaneous, spontaneously
curious, curiously
complete, completely
hideous, hideously
obvious, obviously
usual, usually
sad, sadly
final, finally

Page 18 • Alphabetical Order

behave	guard	pattern
bright	height	poison
chase	history	section
classic	impress	stolen
disaster	interval	umbrella
drawer	laughter	under
enjoyment	level	zebra
every	open	zinc
grammar	oven	

Page 19 • Write the Words

words written as neatly as possible

Brain Booster:

island

Page 20 • Progress Test 3

1. favourite
2. submarine
3. national
4. comical
5. earth
6. beautiful
7. grammar
8. height
9. bright
10. disagree
11. experiment
12. consideration
13. completely
14. finally
15. obvious
16. recycle
17. supermarket
18. honest
19. strength
20. section

Page 21 • Tricky Words

angriness	enjoyment
angrily	enjoyable
	enjoyably
possibly	unenjoyable
impossible	
impossibly	happiness
	happily
	unhappy
	tidiness
	tidily
	untidy

Page 22 • Practise the Words

words written as neatly as possible

naughty
politician
increase
mathematician
heard

Page 23 • Pair the Words

relevant, irrelevant
regular, irregular
correct, incorrect
mature, immature
legal, illegal
possible, impossible
responsible, irresponsible
patient, impatient
active, inactive

Page 24 • Alphabetical Order

agent	moment
attitude	perfect
creation	plenty
custard	popular
depth	present
describe	reverse
different	royal
drift	special
energy	straight
exercise	tonight
kindly	tremendous
knock	yacht
manage	yesterday

Page 25 • Write the Words

words written as neatly as possible

Brain Booster:
fraction

Page 26 • Progress Test 4

1.	naughty	11.	energy
2.	regular	12.	recently
3.	possibly	13.	different
4.	tidiness	14.	correct
5.	promise	15.	popular
6.	important	16.	enjoyable
7.	musician	17.	sentence
8.	happiness	18.	patient
9.	remember	19.	active
10.	attitude	20.	heard

Page 27 • Sort the Words

shiny	adoring
	adored
sensing	adoration
sensed	
sensation	informing
	informed
clockwise	information
anticlockwise	
	autobiography
	autograph

Page 28 • Write the Words

words written as neatly as possible

treasure
furniture
creature
measure
adventure

Brain Booster:
natural, naturally, or any other appropriate word

Page 29 • Pair the Words

natural, naturally
basic, basically
septic, antiseptic
simple, simply
humble, humbly
noble, nobly
social, antisocial
frantic, frantically
dramatic, dramatically

Page 30 • Alphabetical Order

always	library
animal	often
cinema	otherwise
couple	perfect
energetic	practical
exhausted	season
heart	shoulder
horrible	toast
ideal	tremble
italic	waiting
journey	weight
junior	wireless
length	worry

Page 31 • Write the Words

words written as neatly as possible

Brain Booster:
bought, caught, or any other rhyming word

Page 32 • Progress Test 5

1. nature
2. junior
3. rein
4. reign
5. weather
6. whether
7. dramatically
8. shiny
9. adore
10. gentle
11. library
12. measure
13. clockwise
14. antisocial
15. simple
16. pleasure
17. furniture
18. cinema
19. practical
20. information

Page 33 • Sort the Words

reaction, inaction
completed, completing, completion, completely
invented, inventing, inventive, invention, inventor
injecting, injected, injection
hesitated, hesitating, hesitation

Page 34 • Write the Words

words written as neatly as possible

antique
league
science
neighbour

Brain Booster:
uniquely

Page 35 • Homophones

piece, peace
meet, meat
male, mail
brake, break
plain, plane
fair, fare
not, knot
main, mane
meddle, medal

Page 36 • Alphabetical Order

active	notice
article	pendant
cement	property
conversation	radio
diamond	reduce
during	sample
forehead	scroll
frighten	timber
launch	topical
lightning	weather
mistake	whether
myself	yearly
natural	youthful

Page 37 • Write the Words

words written as neatly as possible

Brain Booster:
choruses

Page 38 • Progress Test 6

1. neighbour	11. hesitate
2. injected	12. piece
3. machine	13. peace
4. notice	14. meddle
5. inventor	15. brake
6. conversation	16. chorus
7. completion	17. antique
8. lightning	18. decorate
9. character	19. science
10. tongue	20. radio

Page 39 • Sort the Words

divided	invaded
dividing	invading
division	invasion
confused	decided
confusing	deciding
confusion	decision
	collided
	colliding
	collision
	televised
	televising
	television

Page 40 • Practise the Words

words written as neatly as possible

jealous
mountain
enormous
famous

Brain Booster:
dangerously

Page 41 • Pair the Words

prepare, preparation
music, musical
courage, courageous
magic, magical
vigour, vigorous
usual, unusual
glamour, glamorous
outrage, outrageous
admire, admiration

Page 42 • Alphabetical Order

already	interesting
artistic	material
blackberry	middle
broken	opposite
city	ordinary
complete	pause
daughter	phoneme
discuss	revise
early	runner
enough	viaduct
given	vocabulary
glasses	yawning
imagine	yourself

Page 43 • Apostrophes

words written as neatly as possible

Brain Booster:
nurses'

Page 44 • Progress Test 7

1. yourself
2. enormous
3. confusion
4. interesting
5. invasion
6. televised
7. material
8. girl's
9. girls'
10. artistic
11. unusual
12. baby's
13. babies'
14. humour
15. mountains
16. courage
17. jealous
18. dangerous
19. prepare
20. decision

Well done!
See you next time.